Embrace the unique beauty of circular afghans!
These four designs by Sharon H. Silverman are all easy to crochet with medium or bulky weight yarns.

I0879235

LEISURE ARTS, INC.
Maumelle, Arkansas

EASY +

Finished Size:
Approximately 48" (122 cm) diameter

Heritage *Swirl*

SHOPPING LIST

Yarn (Medium Weight) MEDIUM 4

[6 ounces, 315 yards
(170.1 grams, 288 meters) per skein]:

- ☐ Gold - 1 skein
- ☐ Rose - 1 skein
- ☐ Brown - 1 skein
- ☐ Green - 1 skein

Crochet Hook

- ☐ Size I (5.5 mm)
  or size needed for gauge

GAUGE INFORMATION

In pattern, 10 sts = 4" (10 cm);
7 rnds = 4½" (11.5 cm)

Gauge Swatch: 7" (17.75 cm) from point to point

Work same as Afghan through Rnd 4: 56 dc.

AFGHAN

With Gold, ch 6; join with slip st to form a ring.

Rnd 1 (Right side)**:** Ch 5 **(first 2 chs count as first hdc)**, sc in third ch from hook, work 2 dc around first hdc, ★ hdc in ring, ch 3, sc in third ch from hook, work 2 dc around post of last hdc made; repeat from ★ 6 times **more**; join with slip st to ch at base of first sc, finish off: 32 sts (8 points).

Note: Loop a short piece of yarn around any stitch to mark Rnd 1 as **right** side.

Rnd 2: With **right** side facing, join Rose with slip st in same st as joining; ch 3 **(counts as one dc, now and throughout)**, dc in same ch and in next 3 sts, ★ slip st in ch at base of next sc, ch 3, dc in same ch and in next 3 sts; repeat from ★ around; join with slip st to same st as first slip st, finish off: 40 dc.

Rnd 3: With **right** side facing, join Gold with slip st in first dc on any point; ch 3, dc in same st and in next 4 dc, ★ slip st in first dc on next point, ch 3, dc in same st and in next 4 dc; repeat from ★ around; join with slip st to same st as first slip st, finish off: 48 dc.

Rnd 4: With **right** side facing, join Brown with slip st in first dc on any point; ch 3, dc in same st and in next 5 dc, ★ slip st in first dc on next point, ch 3, dc in same st and in next 5 dc; repeat from ★ around; join with slip st to same st as first slip st, finish off: 56 dc.

Rnd 5: With **right** side facing, join Gold with slip st in first dc on any point; ch 3, dc in same st and in each dc across same point, ★ slip st in first dc on next point, ch 3, dc in same st and in each dc across same point; repeat from ★ around; join with slip st to same st as first slip st, finish off: 64 dc.

Rnd 6: With Green, repeat Rnd 5: 72 dc.

Rnd 7: Repeat Rnd 5: 80 dc.

Rnd 8: With **right** side facing, join Rose with slip st in first dc on any point; ch 3, dc in same st and in each dc across same point, ★ slip st in first dc on next point, ch 3, dc in same st and in each dc across same point; repeat from ★ around; join with slip st to same st as first slip st, do **not** finish off: 88 dc.

Rnd 9: Slip st to top of first dc of first point, ch 3, dc in same st and in each dc across same point, ★ slip st in first dc on next point, ch 3, dc in same st and in each dc across same point; repeat from ★ around; join with slip st to same st as joining slip st, finish off: 96 dc.

Rnd 10: Repeat Rnd 5: 104 dc.

Rnds 11 and 12: With Brown, repeat Rnds 8 and 9: 120 dc.

Rnd 13: Repeat Rnd 5: 128 dc.

Rnds 14 and 15: With Green, repeat Rnds 8 and 9: 144 dc.

Rnd 16: Repeat Rnd 5: 152 dc.

Rnd 17: Repeat Rnd 8: 160 dc.

Rnd 18: Slip st to top of first dc of first point, ch 3, dc in same st and in each dc across same point, ★ slip st in first dc on next point, ch 3, dc in same st and in each dc across same point; repeat from ★ around; join with slip st to same st as first slip st, do **not** finish off: 168 dc.

Rnd 19: Repeat Rnd 9: 176 dc.

Rnd 20: Repeat Rnd 5: 184 dc.

Rnds 21-23: With Brown, repeat Rnds 17-19: 208 dc.

Rnd 24: Repeat Rnd 5: 216 dc.

Rnds 25-27: With Green, repeat Rnds 17-19: 240 dc.

Rnd 28: Repeat Rnd 5: 248 dc.

Rnd 29: Repeat Rnd 8: 256 dc.

Rnds 30 and 31: Repeat Rnd 18 twice: 272 dc.

Rnd 32: Repeat Rnd 9: 280 dc.

Rnd 33: Repeat Rnd 5: 288 dc.

Rnds 34-37: With Brown, repeat Rnds 29-32: 320 dc.

Rnd 38: With **right** side facing, join Gold with sc in first dc on any point ***(see Joining With Sc, page 30)***; sc in next 14 dc, hdc in next 15 dc, dc in next 10 dc, ★ sc in next 15 dc, hdc in next 15 dc, dc in next 10 dc; repeat from ★ around; join with slip st to first sc.

Rnds 39 and 40: Ch 1, sc in same st as joining and in each st around; join with slip st to first sc.

Finish off.

EASY

Finished Size:
Approximately 60" (152.5 cm) in diameter

Promising *Skies*

SHOPPING LIST

Yarn (Medium Weight) 4 MEDIUM

[4 ounces, 204 yards

(113.4 grams, 186 meters) per skein]:

☐ 7 skeins

Crochet Hook

☐ Size H (5 mm)

or size needed for gauge

GAUGE INFORMATION

Rnds 1-4 = 5½" (14 cm)

Gauge Swatch: 4" (10 cm) diameter

Work same as Afghan through Rnd 3: 36 dc and 6 ch-1 sps.

STITCH GUIDE

TREBLE CROCHET ***(abbreviated tr)***

YO twice, insert hook in st or sp indicated, YO and pull up a loop (4 loops on hook), (YO and draw through 2 loops on hook) 3 times.

DOUBLE TREBLE CROCHET ***(abbreviated dtr)***

YO 3 times, insert hook in sc indicated, YO and pull up a loop (5 loops on hook), (YO and draw through 2 loops on hook) 4 times.

TRIPLE TREBLE CROCHET ***(abbreviated tr tr)***

YO 4 times, insert hook in sc indicated, YO and pull up a loop (6 loops on hook), (YO and draw through 2 loops on hook) 5 times.

2-DOUBLE CROCHET CLUSTER ***(abbreviated 2-dc Cluster)*** (uses one st)

★ YO, insert hook in st indicated, YO and pull up a loop, YO and draw through 2 loops on hook; repeat from ★ once **more**, YO and draw all 3 loops on hook.

5-DOUBLE CROCHET CLUSTER ***(abbreviated 5-dc Cluster)*** (uses one ch-2 sp)

★ YO, insert hook in ch-2 sp indicated, YO and pull up a loop, YO and draw through 2 loops on hook; repeat from ★ 4 times **more**, YO and draw through 5 loops on hook, YO and draw through remaining 2 loops on hook.

DOUBLE CROCHET 2 TOGETHER ***(abbreviated dc2tog)*** (uses next 2 sc)

★ YO, insert hook in **next** sc, YO and pull up a loop, YO and draw through 2 loops on hook; repeat from ★ once **more**, YO and draw through all 3 loops on hook.

DOUBLE CROCHET 5 TOGETHER

(abbreviated dc5tog)

(uses next 5 dc)

★ YO, insert hook in **next** dc, YO and pull up a loop, YO and draw through 2 loops on hook; repeat from ★ 4 times **more**, YO and draw through 5 loops on hook, YO and draw through remaining 2 loops on hook.

DOUBLE CROCHET 6 TOGETHER

(abbreviated dc6tog)

(uses next 6 dc)

★ YO, insert hook in **next** dc, YO and pull up a loop, YO and draw through 2 loops on hook; repeat from ★ 5 times **more**, YO and draw through 6 loops on hook, YO and draw through remaining 2 loops on hook.

PICOT

Ch 3, slip st in third ch from hook.

AFGHAN

Ch 6; join with slip st to form a ring.

Rnd 1 (Right side)**:** Ch 3 **(counts as first dc, now and throughout)**, 11 dc in ring; join with slip st to first dc: 12 dc.

Rnd 2: [Ch 2, dc in same st as joining **(counts as first 2-dc Cluster, now and throughout)**], ch 5, skip next dc, ★ work 2-dc Cluster in next dc, ch 5, skip next dc; repeat from ★ around; join with slip st to first 2-dc Cluster: 6 2-dc Clusters and 6 ch-5 sps.

Rnd 3: (Slip st, ch 3, 5 dc) in next ch-5 sp, ch 1, (6 dc in next ch-5 sp, ch 1) around; join with slip st to first dc: 36 dc and 6 ch-1 sps.

Rnd 4: Ch 3, dc in next 2 dc, ch 2, dc in next 3 dc, ch 2, skip next ch-1 sp, ★ dc in next 3 dc, ch 2, dc in next 3 dc, ch 2, skip next ch-1 sp; repeat from ★ around; join with slip st to first dc: 36 dc and 12 ch-2 sps.

Rnd 5: Ch 3, dc in next 2 dc, work 5-dc Cluster in next ch-2 sp, dc in next 3 dc, ch 5, ★ dc in next 3 dc, work 5-dc Cluster in next ch-2 sp, dc in next 3 dc, ch 5; repeat from ★ around; join with slip st to first dc: 36 dc, 6 5-dc Clusters, and 6 ch-5 sps.

Rnd 6: Ch 3, dc in next 2 dc, skip next 5-dc Cluster, dc in next 3 dc, ch 4, sc in next ch-5 sp, ch 4, ★ dc in next 3 dc, skip next 5-dc Cluster, dc in next 3 dc, ch 4, sc in next ch-5 sp, ch 4; repeat from ★ around; join with slip st to first dc: 36 dc, 6 sc, and 12 ch-4 sps.

Rnd 7: Ch 2, dc5tog, (ch 6, sc in next ch-4 sp) twice, ★ ch 6, dc6tog, (ch 6, sc in next ch-4 sp) twice; repeat from ★ around; ch 3, skip beginning ch-2 and dc in top of dc5tog to form last ch-6 sp: 18 ch-6 sps.

Rnd 8: Ch 1, sc in last ch-6 sp made, ch 7, (sc in next ch-6 sp, ch 7) around; join with slip st to first sc: 18 ch-7 sps.

Rnd 9: (Slip st, ch 3, 10 dc) in first ch-7 sp, sc in next ch-7 sp, (11 dc in next ch-7 sp, sc in next ch-7 sp) around; join with slip st to first dc: 99 dc and 9 sc.

Rnd 10: Ch 1, sc in same st as joining and in next 4 dc, (sc, ch 12, sc) in next dc, ★ sc in next 5 dc, (sc, ch 12, sc) in next st; repeat from ★ around; join with slip st to first sc: 126 sc and 18 loops.

Rnd 11: Slip st in next sc, ch 1, sc in next 2 sc, skip next 2 sc, [slip st in next loop, ch 3 **(counts as one dc, now and throughout)**], (16 dc, slip st) in same loop, skip next 3 sc, sc in next 2 sc, ★ skip next 2 sc, (slip st, ch 3, 16 dc, slip st) in next loop, skip next 3 sc, sc in next 2 sc; repeat from ★ around to last 2 sc, skip last 2 sc; join with slip st to first sc: 306 dc (18 17-dc groups).

Rnd 12: Slip st in first 8 sts, ch 1, sc in next dc, (ch 5, skip next dc, sc in next dc) twice, ★ ch 10, skip next 6 dc of next 17-dc group, sc in next dc, (ch 5, skip next dc, sc in next dc) twice; repeat from ★ around, ch 5, dtr in first sc to form last loop: 36 ch-5 sps and 18 loops.

Rnd 13: Ch 4 **(counts as first tr, now and throughout)**, (2 dc, 2 hdc, 2 sc) in last loop made, sc in next ch-5 sp, ch 8, sc in next ch-5 sp, ★ (2 sc, 2 hdc, 2 dc, tr, 2 dc, 2 hdc, 2 sc) in next loop, sc in next ch-5 sp, ch 8, sc in next ch-5 sp; repeat from ★ around, (2 sc, 2 hdc, 2 dc) in same loop as first tr; join with slip st to first tr: 270 sts and 18 ch-8 sps.

Rnd 14: Ch 1, sc in same st as joining, ch 10, dc in next ch-8 sp, ★ ch 10, skip next 7 sts, sc in next tr, ch 10, dc in next ch-8 sp; repeat from ★ around to last 7 sts, ch 5, skip last 7 sts, dtr in first sc to form last loop: 36 loops.

Rnd 15: Ch 4, (2 dc, 2 hdc, 2 sc) in last loop made, (2 sc, 2 hdc, 2 dc, tr, 2 dc, 2 hdc, 2 sc) in next loop and in each loop around, (2 sc, 2 hdc, 2 dc) in same loop as first tr; join with slip st to first tr: 468 sts.

Rnd 16: Ch 1, sc in same st as joining, ★ ch 10, skip next 12 sts, sc in next tr; repeat from ★ around to last 12 sts, ch 5, skip last 12 sts, dtr in first sc to form last loop: 36 loops.

Rnd 17: Repeat Rnd 15: 468 sts.

Rnd 18: Ch 2, dc in same st as joining, ch 6, skip next 5 sts, dc2tog, ch 6, skip next 5 sts, ★ work 2-dc Cluster in next tr, ch 6, skip next 5 sts, dc2tog, ch 6, skip next 5 sts; repeat from ★ around; join with slip st to first 2-dc Cluster: 72 ch-6 sps.

Rnd 19: (Slip st, ch 3, 4 dc) in next ch-6 sp, (ch 1, 5 dc in next ch-6 sp) around, sc in first dc to form last ch-1 sp: 360 dc and 72 ch-1 sps.

Rnd 20: Ch 1, sc in last ch-1 sp made, (ch 12, sc in next ch-1 sp) around; ch 6, tr tr in first sc to form last loop: 72 loops.

Rnd 21 and 22: Ch 1, sc in last ch-12 loop made, (ch 12, sc in next ch-12 loop) around; ch 6, tr tr in first sc to form last loop.

Rnd 23: Ch 1, sc in last loop made, 11 dc in next loop, (sc in next loop, 11 dc in next loop) around; join with slip st to first sc: 432 sts.

Rnd 24: Ch 1, (sc, ch 12, sc) in same st as joining, sc in next 5 dc, ★ (sc, ch 12, sc) in next st, sc in next 5 dc; repeat from ★ around; join with slip st to first sc: 72 loops.

Rnd 25: ★ (Slip st, ch 3, 16 dc, slip st) in next loop, skip next 3 sc, sc in next 2 sc, skip next 2 sc; repeat from ★ around; join with slip st to first slip st: 72 17-dc groups.

Rnds 26 and 27: Repeat Rnds 12 and 13: 72 ch-8 sps.

Rnd 28: Ch 1, sc in same st as joining, ch 7, dc in next ch-8 sp, ★ ch 7, skip next 7 sts, sc in next tr, ch 7, dc in next ch-8 sp; repeat from ★ around to last 7 sts, ch 3, skip last 7 sts, tr in first sc to form last ch-7 sp: 144 ch-7 sps.

Rnds 29 and 30: Ch 1, sc in last ch-7 sp made, (ch 7, sc in next ch-7 sp) around, ch 3, tr in first sc to form last ch-7 sp.

Rnd 31: Ch 3, 2 dc in last ch-7 sp made, (ch 1, 3 dc in next ch-7 sp) around, sc in first dc to form last ch-1 sp: 432 dc and 144 ch-1 sps.

Rnd 32: Ch 1, sc in last ch-1 sp made, ch 7, sc in next ch-1 sp, skip next dc, sc in next dc, skip next dc, ★ sc in next ch-1 sp, ch 7, sc in next ch-1 sp, skip next dc, sc in next dc, skip next dc; repeat from ★ around; join with slip st to first sc: 216 sc and 72 ch-7 sps.

Rnd 33: Slip st in next ch-7 sp, ch 1, (2 sc, 2 hdc, 2 dc, tr, Picot, 2 dc, 2 hdc, 2 sc) in same sp, skip next sc, sc in next sc, skip next sc, ★ (2 sc, 2 hdc, 2 dc, tr, Picot, 2 dc, 2 hdc, 2 sc) in next ch-7 sp, skip next sc, sc in next sc, skip next sc; repeat from ★ around; join with slip st to first sc, finish off.

EASY +

Finished Size:
Approximately 62½" (159 cm) diameter

Rainbow *Wedges*

SHOPPING LIST

Yarn (Medium Weight) MEDIUM 4

[6 ounces, 315 yards (170.1 grams, 288 meters) per skein]:

- ☐ Red -1 skein
- ☐ Orange - 1 skein
- ☐ Gold - 1 skein
- ☐ Yellow - 1 skein
- ☐ Lt Green - 1 skein
- ☐ Green - 1 skein
- ☐ Blue - 1 skein
- ☐ Dk Blue - 1 skein
- ☐ Lt Lavender - 1 skein
- ☐ Lavender - 1 skein
- ☐ Purple - 1 skein

Crochet Hook

- ☐ Size J (6 mm) **or** size needed for gauge

Additional Supplies

- ☐ Yarn needle

GAUGE INFORMATION

In pattern,

11 sts and 6 rows = 4" (10 cm)

Gauge Swatch: 4" wide x 6" high (10 cm x 15.25 cm)

Ch 12.

Row 1 (Right side)**:** Sc in second ch from hook and in each ch across: 11 sc.

Rows 2-7: Work same as Wedge: 5 dc.

Rows 8 and 9: Work same as Wedge Rows 46 and 47.

STITCH GUIDE

CLUSTER (uses one st)

★ YO, insert hook in st indicated, YO and pull up a loop, YO and draw through 2 loops on hook; repeat from ★ 4 times **more** (6 loops on hook), YO and draw through 5 loops on hook, YO and draw through remaining 2 loops on hook.

CLUSTER DECREASE (uses next 2 sts)

[YO, **insert** hook in **next** st, YO and pull up a loop, YO and draw through 2 loops on hook] twice, ★ YO, insert hook in **same** st, YO and pull up a loop, YO and draw through 2 loops on hook; repeat from ★ 3 times **more** (7 loops on hook), YO and draw through 5 loops on hook, YO and draw through remaining 3 loops on hook.

DOUBLE CROCHET 2 TOGETHER ***(abbreviated dc2tog)*** (uses next ch-1 sp and next Cluster)

YO, insert hook in next ch-1 sp, YO and pull up a loop, YO and draw through 2 loops on hook, YO, insert hook in top of next Cluster, YO and pull up a loop, YO and draw through 2 loops on hook, YO and draw through remaining 3 loops on hook **(counts as one dc)**.

WEDGE (Make 11 total, one **each** color)

Ch 50.

Row 1 (Right side)**:** Sc in second ch from hook and in each ch across: 49 sc.

Note: Loop a short piece of yarn around any stitch to mark Row 1 as **right** side.

Row 2: Ch 3 **(counts as first dc, now and throughout)**, turn; work Cluster decrease, ch 1, ★ skip next sc, work Cluster in next sc, ch 1; repeat from ★ across to last 2 sc, skip next sc, dc in last sc: 25 sts and 23 ch-1 sps.

Row 3: Ch 3, turn; dc2tog, dc in next ch-1 sp and in each st and each ch-1 sp across: 47 dc.

Row 4: Ch 3, turn; work Cluster decrease, ch 1, ★ skip next dc, work Cluster in next dc, ch 1; repeat from ★ across to last 2 dc, skip next dc, dc in last dc: 24 sts and 22 ch-1 sps.

Rows 5-45: Repeat Rows 3 and 4, 20 times; then repeat Row 3 once **more**: 5 dc.

Row 46: Ch 3, turn; work Cluster decrease, ch 1, skip next dc, dc in last dc: 3 sts and one ch-1 sp.

Row 47: Ch 2, turn; dc2tog, dc in last dc; finish off.

FINISHING

Using photo as guide, weave Wedges together as follows: Using corresponding color yarn, with **right** sides of both pieces facing you and edges even, sew through both sides once to secure the seam, leaving an ample yarn end to weave in later. Insert the needle from **right** to **left** through one strand on each piece ***(Fig. A)***. Bring the needle around and insert it from **right** to **left** through the next strand on both pieces. Continue in this manner across, matching rows.

Fig. A

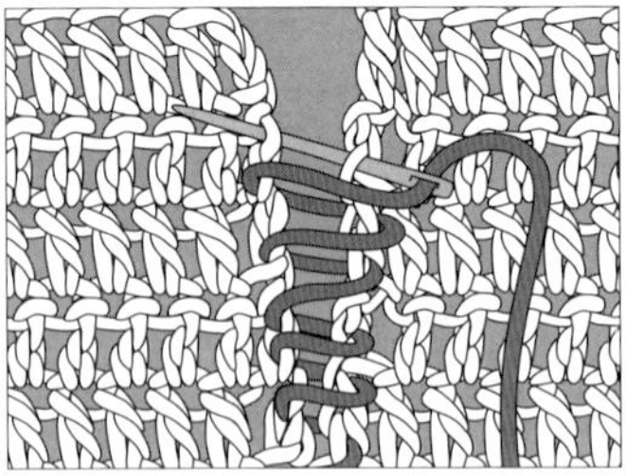

There will be a small hole left at the center of the afghan once all the Wedges are woven together.

TRIM

With **right** side facing and working in free loops of beginning ch on each Wedge ***(Fig. B)***, join Purple with sc in any ch ***(see Joining With Sc, page 30)***; sc in each ch around; join with slip st to first sc, finish off.

Fig. B

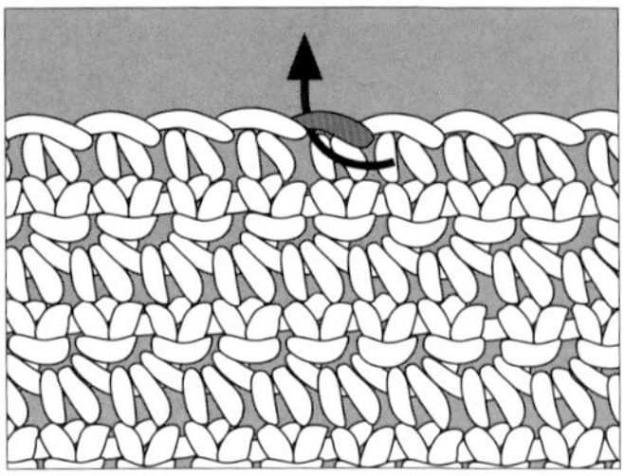

CENTER

With Red, ch 4; join with slip st to form a ring.

Rnd 1 (Right side)**:** Ch 3, 11 dc in ring; join with slip st to first dc: 12 dc.

Note: Mark Rnd 1 as **right** side.

Rnd 2: Ch 3, dc in same st as joining, 2 dc in next dc and in each dc around; join with slip st to first dc: 24 dc.

Rnd 3: Ch 3, dc in same st as joining and in next dc, (2 dc in next dc, dc in next dc) around; join with slip st to first dc, finish off leaving a long end for sewing.

With **right** side facing, overlapping ends of Wedges, and using long end, sew Center over center hole, do **not** cut yarn. With **wrong** side facing and using same end, sew Center to sts on Row 47 of each Wedge.

EASY

Finished Size:
Approximately 45" (114.5 cm) diameter

Metropolitan *Flair*

SHOPPING LIST

Yarn (Bulky Weight) BULKY 5

[3.5 ounces,127 yards
(100 grams,116 meters) per skein]:

- ☐ Black - 2 skeins
- ☐ Dk Grey - 2 skeins
- ☐ Lt Grey - 2 skeins
- ☐ Tan - 2 skeins

Crochet Hook

- ☐ Size K (6.5 mm)
  or size needed for gauge

GAUGE INFORMATION

10 dc = 4" (10 cm);
4 rnds = 3" (7.5 cm)

Gauge Swatch: 4" (10 cm) diameter

Work same as Afghan through Rnd 2: 24 dc.

AFGHAN

With Black, ch 4; join with slip st to form a ring.

Rnd 1 (Right side)**:** Ch 3 **(counts as first dc, now and throughout)**, 11 dc in ring; join with slip st to first dc, finish off: 12 dc.

Note: Loop a short piece of yarn around any stitch to mark Rnd 1 as **right** side.

Rnd 2: With **right** side facing, join Dk Grey with dc in any dc ***(see Joining With Dc, page 30)***; dc in same st, 2 dc in next dc and in each dc around; join with slip st to first dc, finish off: 24 dc.

Rnd 3: With **right** side facing, join Black with dc in first dc; 2 dc in next dc, (dc in next dc, 2 dc in next dc) around; join with slip st to first dc, finish off: 36 dc.

Rnd 4: With **right** side facing, join Dk Grey with dc in first dc; dc in same st and in next 2 dc, (2 dc in next dc, dc in next 2 dc) around; join with slip st to first dc, finish off: 48 dc.

Rnd 5: With **right** side facing, join Grey with dc in first dc; dc in same st and in next 3 dc, (2 dc in next dc, dc in next 3 dc) around; join with slip st to first dc, finish off: 60 dc.

Rnd 6: With **right** side facing, join Dk Grey with dc in first dc; dc in same st and in next 4 dc, (2 dc in next dc, dc in next 4 dc) around; join with slip st to first dc, finish off: 72 dc.

Each round increases by 12 dc. In order to keep the piece round, stagger the increases by joining the new yarn for each round between increases, not in a dc of an increase. On each round, there will be one additional dc between the increases.

Using the color sequence as follows, continue in same manner working given number of dc between each increase.

Rnd 7: Lt Grey - 5 dc between each increase: 84 dc.

Rnd 8: Tan - 6 dc between each increase: 96 dc.

Rnd 9: Lt Grey - 7 dc between each increase: 108 dc.

Rnd 10: Tan - 8 dc between each increase: 120 dc.

Rnd 11: Black - 9 dc between each increase: 132 dc.

Rnd 12: Tan - 10 dc between each increase: 144 dc.

Rnd 13: Black - 11 dc between each increase: 156 dc.

Rnd 14: Dk Grey - 12 dc between each increase: 168 dc.

Rnd 15: Black - 13 dc between each increase: 180 dc.

Rnd 16: Dk Grey - 14 dc between each increase: 192 dc.

Rnd 17: Lt Grey - 15 dc between each increase: 204 dc.

Rnd 18: Dk Grey - 16 dc between each increase: 216 dc.

Rnd 19: Lt Grey - 17 dc between each increase: 228 dc.

Rnd 20: Tan - 18 dc between each increase: 240 dc.

Rnd 21: Lt Grey - 19 dc between each increase: 252 dc.

Rnd 22: Tan - 20 dc between each increase: 264 dc.

Rnd 23: Black - 21 dc between each increase: 276 dc.

Rnd 24: Tan - 22 dc between each increase: 288 dc.

Rnd 25: Black - 23 dc between each increase: 300 dc.

Rnd 26: Dk Grey - 24 dc between each increase: 312 dc.

Rnd 27: Black - 25 dc between each increase: 324 dc.

Rnd 28: Dk Grey - 26 dc between each increase: 336 dc.

Rnd 29: Lt Grey - 27 dc between each increase: 348 dc.

Rnd 30: With **right** side facing, join Tan with sc in any dc ***(see Joining With Sc, page 30)***; sc in each dc around; join with slip st to first sc, finish off.

Rnd 31: With **right** side facing, join Black with slip st in any sc, ch 1; working from **left** to **right**, work reverse sc in each st around ***(Figs. 1a-d, page 31)***; join with slip st to first st, finish off.

General Instructions

ABBREVIATIONS

ch(s)	chain(s)
cm	centimeters
dc	double crochet(s)
dc2tog	double crochet 2 together
dc5tog	double crochet 5 together
dc6tog	double crochet 6 together
dtr	double treble crochet(s)
hdc	half double crochet(s)
mm	millimeters
Rnd(s)	Round(s)
sc	single crochet(s)
sp(s)	space(s)
st(s)	stitch(es)
tr	treble crochet(s)
tr tr	triple treble crochet(s)
YO	yarn over

SYMBOLS & TERMS

★ — work instructions following ★ as many **more** times as indicated in addition to the first time.

( ) or **[ ]** — work enclosed instructions **as many** times as specified by the number immediately following **or** work all enclosed instructions in the stitch or space indicated **or** contains explanatory remarks.

colon (:) — the number(s) given after a colon at the end of a row or round denote(s) the number of stitches or spaces you should have on that row or round.

CROCHET TERMINOLOGY		
UNITED STATES		INTERNATIONAL
slip stitch (slip st)	=	single crochet (sc)
single crochet (sc)	=	double crochet (dc)
half double crochet (hdc)	=	half treble crochet (htr)
double crochet (dc)	=	treble crochet (tr)
treble crochet (tr)	=	double treble crochet (dtr)
double treble crochet (dtr)	=	triple treble crochet (ttr)
triple treble crochet (tr tr)	=	quadruple treble crochet (qtr)
skip	=	miss

Yarn Weight Symbol & Names	LACE 0	SUPER FINE 1	FINE 2	LIGHT 3	MEDIUM 4	BULKY 5	SUPER BULKY 6	JUMBO 7
Type of Yarns in Category	Fingering, size 10 crochet thread	Sock, Fingering, Baby	Sport, Baby	DK, Light Worsted	Worsted, Afghan, Aran	Chunky, Craft, Rug	Super Bulky, Roving	Jumbo, Roving
Crochet Gauge* Ranges in Single Crochet to 4" (10 cm)	32-42 sts**	21-32 sts	16-20 sts	12-17 sts	11-14 sts	8-11 sts	6-9 sts	5 sts and fewer
Advised Hook Size Range	Steel*** 6 to 8, Regular hook B-1	B-1 to E-4	E-4 to 7	7 to I-9	I-9 to K-10½	K-10½ to M/N-13	M/N-13 to Q	Q and larger

*GUIDELINES ONLY: The chart above reflects the most commonly used gauges and hook sizes for specific yarn categories.

** Lace weight yarns are usually crocheted with larger hooks to create lacy openwork patterns. Accordingly, a gauge range is difficult to determine. Always follow the gauge stated in your pattern.

*** Steel crochet hooks are sized differently from regular hooks–the higher the number, the smaller the hook, which is the reverse of regular hook sizing.

BEGINNER	Projects for first-time crocheters using basic stitches. Minimal shaping.
EASY	Projects using yarn with basic stitches, repetitive stitch patterns, simple color changes, and simple shaping and finishing.
INTERMEDIATE	Projects using a variety of techniques, such as basic lace patterns or color patterns, mid-level shaping and finishing.
EXPERIENCED	Projects with intricate stitch patterns, techniques and dimension, such as non-repeating patterns, multi-color techniques, fine threads, small hooks, detailed shaping and refined finishing.

CROCHET HOOKS																	
U.S.	B-1	C-2	D-3	E-4	F-5	G-6	7	H-8	I-9	J-10	K-10½	L-11	M/N-13	N/P-15	P/Q	Q	S
Metric - mm	2.25	2.75	3.25	3.5	3.75	4	4.5	5	5.5	6	6.5	8	9	10	15	16	19

GAUGE

Exact gauge is **essential** for proper size. Before beginning your Afghan, make the sample swatch given in the individual instructions in the yarn and hook specified. After completing the swatch, measure it, counting your stitches and rows/rounds carefully. If your swatch is larger or smaller than specified, **make another, changing hook size to get the correct gauge**. Keep trying until you find the size hook that will give you the specified gauge.

JOINING WITH SC

When instructed to join with sc, begin with a slip knot on hook. Insert hook in stitch or space indicated, YO and pull up a loop, YO and draw through both loops on hook.

JOINING WITH DC

When instructed to join with dc, begin with a slip knot on hook. YO, holding loop on hook, insert hook in stitch or space indicated, YO and pull up a loop (3 loops on hook), (YO and draw through 2 loops on hook) twice.

REVERSE SINGLE CROCHET

(abbreviated reverse sc)

Working from **left** to **right**, ★ insert hook in st to right of hook ***(Fig. 1a)***, YO and draw through, under and to left of loop on hook (2 loops on hook) ***(Fig. 1b)***, YO and draw through both loops on hook ***(Fig. 1c)*** **(reverse sc made, *Fig. 1d*)**; repeat from ★ around.

Fig. 1a

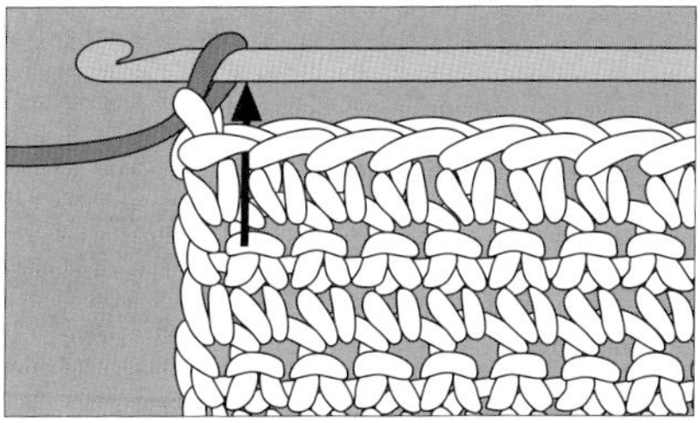

Fig. 1b

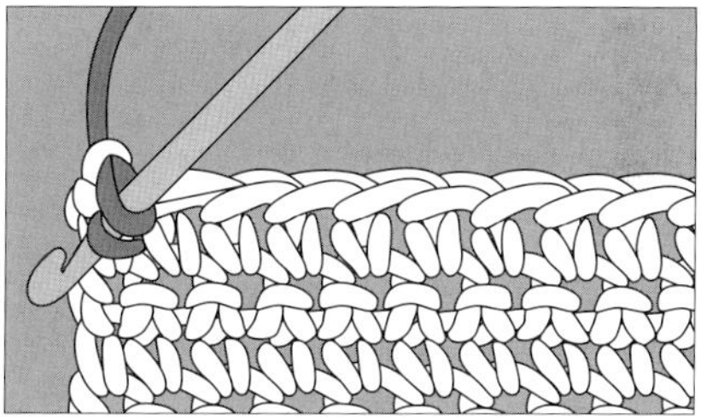

Fig. 1c

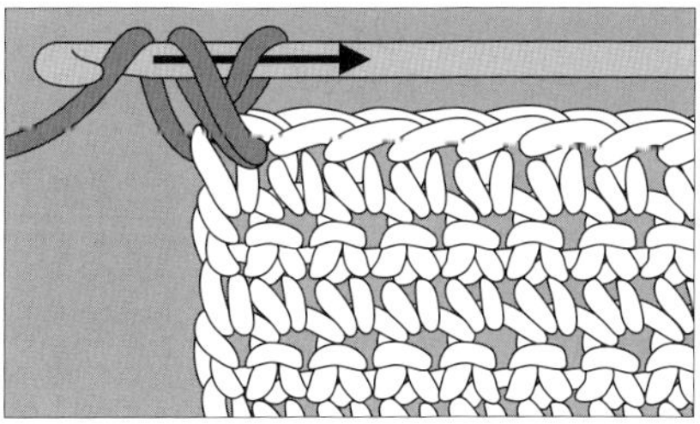

Fig. 1d

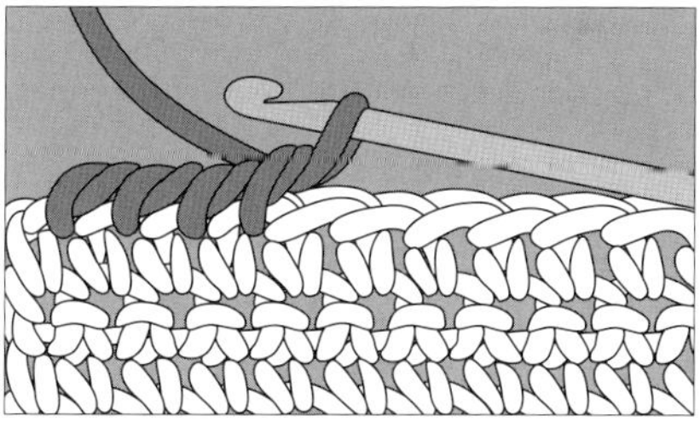

Yarn Information

Afghans in this book were made using various weights of yarn. Any brand of the specified weight of yarn may be used. It is best to refer to the yardage/meters when determining how many balls or skeins to purchase. Remember, to arrive at the finished size, it is the GAUGE/TENSION that is important, not the brand of yarn.

For your convenience, listed below are the specific yarns used to create our photography models. Because yarn manufacturers make frequent changes in their product lines, you may sometimes find it necessary to use a substitute yarn or to search for the discontinued product at alternate suppliers (locally or online).

HERITAGE SWIRL

Caron® Simply Soft®
Gold - #9782 Gold
Rose - #9764 Fuschsia
Brown - #9783 Taupe
Green - #9759 Ocean

PROMISING SKIES

Caron® Simply Soft® Ombre™
#08114 Saturday Blue Jeans

RAINBOW WEDGES

Caron® Simply Soft®
Red - #9763 Harvest Red
Orange - #9778 Orange
Gold - #9782 Gold
Yellow - #9776 Lemonade
Lt Green - #9705 Sage
Green - #9779 Green
Blue - #9784 Cobalt Blue
Dk Blue - #9767 Royal Blue
Lt Lavender - #9717 Orchid
Lavender - #9756 Lavender Blue
Purple - #9781 Purple

METROPOLITAN FLAIR

Lion Brand® Lion's Pride® Woolspun®
Black - #153 Black
Dk Grey - #149 Charcoal
Lt Grey - #150 Oxford Grey
Tan - #099 Linen

We have made every effort to ensure that these instructions are accurate and complete. We cannot, however, be responsible for human error, typographical mistakes, or variations in individual work.

Production Team: Instructional/Technical Editor - Sarah J. Green; Editorial Writer - Susan Frantz Wiles; Senior Graphic Artist - Lora Puls; Graphic Artist - Kellie McAnulty; Photo Stylist - Stephanie Moore; and Photographer - Jason Masters.